Flying Through Cloud

Also by Derek Baines and published by Ginninderra Press
A Most Urgent Task

Derek Baines

Flying Through Cloud

For my father
Raymond Baines
(1922–2003)

Acknowledgements

'Motel Room' was first published in
Ask the Rain (ed. John L. Sheppard), Poets Union, 2004

Words quoted on page 58 are from Toni Morrison's *Sula*, Vintage, 1998

Flying Through Cloud
ISBN 978 1 74027 344 2
Copyright © text Derek Baines 2006
Cover painting: Untitled by Andrew Browne, Oil on Linen,
100cmx100cm, 2003

First published 2006
Reprinted 2016

Ginninderra Press
PO Box 3461 Port Adelaide 5015
www.ginninderrapress.com.au

Contents

Magnolia	7
Recycling	8
The Rock	9
Sunset With Surfboard	10
Heat Haze In Broke	11
Coffee At Brooklyn	12
Essington Park Autumn	13
Following Like Sheep	15
Rainforest	16
Fragile City	18
Birds	19
[Exit] Urban Life	20
Preparing For New Year Celebrations New York	21
Good Wine On a Silver Tray	23
Flying Through Cloud #1	24
Flying Through Cloud #2	25
Flying Through Cloud #3	26
Flying Through Cloud #4	27
Flying Through Cloud #5	28
Last Flight	29
What Size Do You Take In a Jane Debster?	30
The Tracksuit Times	31
Junk Food Attack From Outer Space	34
Early Retirement	36
Coffeehouse Chain	39
The Lawyers	40
Motel Room	42
Artist's Studio	44
Picasso – A Woman Ironing	46
Graffiti	47

Lines of Communication	48
Ten Years	50
Family Reunion	52
That Summer	53
A Neptune Man	54
Countdown	56
Swimmer In the Sea Baths	57
Chopping Vegies For the Stew	58
Charlton Boys	59
The 1960s As Ancient History	61
Headlights of Loss	62
To Write Like Toni Morrison	63
After *Men At Work* – Graham Greene	64
After *The Loved One* – Evelyn Waugh	65
After *Dusty Answer* – Rosamund Lehmann	66
I'm Sure It Was Jan Morris	67
Summer Holiday From Writing School	68
Foreigner Learns Tea	69
Public Library	70
Separation	72
Phyl and Roy	73
Birthday	75
Friendship	76
When Your Lover Is Happy	77
When Your Lover Is Unhappy	78
Au Revoir	79
Delicate Child of Day	80

Magnolia

A hundred baby galahs
choreographed in sleep
already showered
in the morning dew.

Recycling

A veil of angophora leaves
crocheted by nature
in front of the television
filters the blue sky
of the morning
and the still-muscled
pink boughs
are kept warm.

The ageing strongman
of the forest,
sap stains on the bark
of its trousers,
stands its ground.

Inside, a colony of termites
makes its cancerous advance.

Soon, in a high wind or fire,
it will be felled,
realising the inspired plan
contrived by nature
back in the days before radio.

The Rock

A salt lake is watched over
by desert oaks
optimistic that after sixty years,
thin roots will find the water table.
Only then will they be able
to stand worriless
and fill out gangly
adolescent frames.

In this light
scales of rust hang
on the rock –
a flaking barbecue plate
left for centuries without use.

Under the waves of sandstone
upended in midair
the pouch of the hare wallaby formed,
nurturing mother of the stories.

Dark mouldy tracks
mark the place of the Lungkata tale
of ash and smoke
from a hunter's fire,
lit to kill a gluttonous blue-tongue
which stole his prey.

The Middle Kingdom
of all life, all legends.
sunrise and set gives to white folk
new imaginings each day
of laughing lips, an elephant's head,
honeycomb, and eagle's nest.

Sunset With Surfboard

I was too exhausted to notice
after eight hours straight in the waves at Cronulla,
but my poet mate Johnno
said the shadow I was casting that afternoon
looked like I was clutching
a giant knife by its blade.

Taller than I by at least a head,
it had sure cut through
those fleshy rolls of surf for most of the day
until the sun almost set on our work
and, like me by that point,
had begun to need sharpening
for another day of hard labour in the water.

Heat Haze In Broke

Heat haze blurs the view
of vast plains of nothingness
and makes one question
his drunken eyesight.

Bushfire smoke has settled
to rest on the hill slopes
which make the three walls of Broke –
not yet ready to be moved on
like a vagrant unwanted
in our proud town.

First settled 1824
Population 400

Grass crunches underfoot –
the sound of pebbles
not the soft juicy shoots
that would make cows smile
if they could.

Irrigation pipes exposed
on the river bank are dormant
in the drought –
thick black snakes taking in the sun.

Movement of rusty sludge
in the river bed
might only be insects dive-bombing
and forcing a ripple.

Eyes burnt with haze
All smell suspended
in the jail of heat.

Coffee At Brooklyn

Tranquil spring morning at Brooklyn
uninterrupted by commerce
wraps two visitors in a warm suspense.

Antique shop, newsagent, and hotel
all advertise 'fresh bait' in windows,
but doors firmly locked.

Fishing must be an afternoon pursuit here
and the night-life vivid.

An elderly resident pulls
a shopping cart
easily up the hill

We follow
hoping we'll be lead to coffee

Our Pied Piper with the squeaky wheel
turns into her yard and disappears

Buyers with no sellers,
we are eager to consume,
caught in a limbo of civic sleepiness
unconcerned for the appetites
of guests.

Essington Park Autumn

A cover of western sun
fits over the veranda
of the shearers' quarters.

Blue-tongue lizard
hisses inside a length of old pipe,
disturbed by footsteps
rare since the last shearers departed.

The north-east wind
delivers a storm cloud wave
about to break on turned backs

Lucy Humphries quietly watches
afternoon shadows move up the hill
on the opposite side of the creek –
earlier today than yesterday.

Hundreds of Santa Claus spores
from the thistle weed
in the next paddock
dance up and down above the girl,
a puppet show of good luck
for the soul
released after her fifth Christmas.

She giggles at the city folk
come to pick blackberries
in the gully –
of course they have thorns,
didn't you know?
And before you ask, no,
you can't eat the apples,
they are ornamental quince.

Lucy smiles at the visitors
and the rain and the sun –
happy child and wise,
for a hundred and forty years.

Her friend paints these pictures.

Following Like Sheep

Unused to the sight
and determination
of a writer with notebook,
the fatted lamb scared,
dances and leaps,
and with one look back
at the woollen family,
starts an alarmed bleating
echoing across the valley

Relatives follow up
to high ground
on the opposite side,
able to see me finish
and close the book,
also watching
for the hidden wolves.

Rainforest

Rainbow Serpent created
the rivers and waterfalls
tourists now admire
from safe viewing platforms
on a rainforest walk,
guided by signs
in five languages
and the rehearsed words
of the ranger –
every thirty minutes.

Cable car offering
an aerial view
only ever available to birds
and tree-hugging insects,
never sharing their insights.

Panorama underneath –
forest rich green
and tight as broccoli steaming
on the summer stove.

Trees and vines
social climbing
strangling weak competitors,
lest they lose their
daily minute in the sun.

History of the forest
held as a secret
guarded by kauri sentinels
unspeaking for three hundred years.

On the border of the forest
as we head down
to the coast,
fortress walls crack
to reveal brave
patches of grass.

Fragile City

A dusty sky was stirred
spattering with brown
the blue canvas
being admired by the gallery-goers
for its simplicity and perfect shading.
Its purity had dissolved from sight
the telegraph poles,
apartments built
on corrupt payments
and potholed roads
ignored and lonely
despite the constant touch
of heavy traffic.

The wind storm
began an invasion march
through the weaker parts of town
made of wood and tile
Gracious trees standing upright
like solid-trunked old ladies
at the bus stop
boughs outstretched
Nothing could move them
except this whirlwind
carrying the life and toil
of the town with it

Concrete mountains –
office towers reinforced with steel –
seemed indestructible
to all but the terrorist of nature,
which saw them as targets –
If not this time then the next.

Birds

The ten-metre platform was perfectly tempered,
accepting the spring test administered
by a pair of seasoned diver's legs.

Thrown into competition as a small child,
there was never any rehearsal,
no warming-up,
only the race.

His mother watched from the sidelines once,
quietly confident in his ability.
But no cheering.
Then she left home.

A mental starting siren sounded.
There would have been anticipation
if there were an audience.

Microchip muscles wired into sinews
received the signal to move.

A pair of great black wings rose up
like Dracula's cloak.
Mouth readied on the downward swoop
to taste blood
and flesh of the worm.

[Exit] Urban Life

Loneliness as neighbours are unknown.

Escape to a neighbourless solitude.

Jackhammers on a construction site
Bum cracks grotesquely dancing on
rotund builder's labourers.

Escape to quiet and a much better view.

Paying to see the professionals
play-act the cultural life of old.

Escape to small-town amateurism
more fulfilling if you're a part.

Four-dollar latte enriches café owner
Who will afford a country house first –
merchant banker or barista?

Escape to an espresso-less calm.

In the supine life
the withdrawal headaches will pass.

Neon signs invisible
in the sterilised night sky
their insolent messages
no longer reaching me.

Preparing For New Year Celebrations New York

On New Year's Eve
tourists act as inadvertent road blocks
to the few New Yorkers
who are still navigating the sidewalks
of Fifth, Sixth, and Broadway.

In Times Square,
children and cameras
make slower progress than their owners
as they stop to capture
new neon scenes of colour,
shutters wide open.

A list of all languages on random play –
symbols of a ragged volunteer army
of visitors,
all come to defy
a heightened terror alert.

Safety will be enhanced this year,
the likelihood of a suicide bombing
will be reduced –
the NYPD has borrowed extra metal detectors
from the city's schools.

At Tiffany,
couples of men, women,
and women and men
shop for wedding bands.

At Saks
hundreds following the brass rail
pass the windows in joyous respect
of the traditional Christmas display,
and like a car accident on the freeway,
the spectacle slows the foot traffic
to a crawl.

At the Gotham Book Mart on W47th
second-hand titles are shelved
with the new,
and as it is for the whole city,
history and invention are one
as another new year is announced.

Good Wine On a Silver Tray

I don't feel like a bird
in this 747
Birds are carefree I think
and tire awfully
from their incessant flapping
to maintain lift.

I am filled with thought
brought on by low pressure
and good wine
served on a silver tray.

I sit quite still
No room to flap
even if I were inclined.
Wiggling of toes
not really assisting
our passage.

Flying Through Cloud #1

Mountains of dirty snow slush,
clouds shovelled up
against the side of the sky
so we can fly right through.

Flying Through Cloud #2

From here I can see
a wide clear river,
a channel of sky
carved out by aircraft.

The banks of cloud
holding back the tide
of traffic
and protecting the clean
white airspace
from any further business.

Flying Through Cloud #3

In the earliest of dawn
looking to the east
there is a blue-grey
lunar landscape of cloud

At its edge a widening sea
of yellow
spreading towards us
as the tide of day rises.

Flying Through Cloud #4

White breadcrumb tufts of cloud
suspended above sea:
smooth and sparkling
like ice in the winter sun
of morning over Los Angeles.

Flying Through Cloud #5

Billows of cloud like factory smoke
suddenly eaten by the sun
emerging from the east
for its daily work

And in the distance
a golden beach lapped
by a great ocean of sky

Offshore an uncharted archipelago.

Last Flight

It is a bloody big thrill
hurtling down the runway
at 100 miles per hour on a clear day
with the bold post-thunderstorm sun
behind us pushing.

Then there is all
of Moreton Bay, the islands,
and sand bars
their swirls giving everything
a neapolitan flavour.

For a second can I be him
in a RAAF flying officer's uniform
at the throttle of the DC-3

Where the rays of sun ended
the ashes were scattered yesterday
in a rose garden on his beloved island,
and all day with the family together
the doorbell has been ringing
of its own accord.

What Size Do You Take In a Jane Debster?

The final admission that the pumps
were a size too small was painful
A lifetime of shopping education failed.

No refunds and no returns
on sale items.
The Management.

Six toes with no room to breathe –
concert-goers forced immobile
in the moshpit.

Friends circled around the lunch table
Coffee steaming,
Caffeine fuelling the swapping crescendo
of shopping conquests

What size do you take in a Jane Debster?
I have six toes on each foot
There are only a very few brands which suit.

Her closest friends unaware
of the extra toes before now –
She was always
a very well-balanced girl.
Six toes
It's no wonder.

Six toes? Oh I see
Don't worry
we'll take you to a little place
we know in the lane
They do bespoke.

The Tracksuit Times

The design said peel it off
when you warm up
ready for the race

Now the headline could be:
Moulded on
Like Skin Fused
in a House Fire
Pealing could be
dangerous

There is no longer competition
for many;
A spiralling slow-down,
An anti-race

Today in *The Tracksuit Times*
Exclusive shots
of the winter catwalk shows
The finest fabric blends
Teasing Texture
A clamour of unmatched
colours

Grand prize for the most
stretched –
doing its heroic best
to hold together in the absence
of underwear and against the
swinging of the dick
on its freedom march
down the runway.

Most elegant formal tracksuit
of 2002 –
Major competition launch!
Win matching
designer tracksuits
for you and your
entire family

Parliament in uproar:
Prime Minister Breaks
Last Taboo –
Grey Trackies
during Question Time

Tonight on Channel 13
Reality TV Tracksuit-cam
Who will you vote out
of their suit?

Accessorise Carefully:
How to Choose
the Right Ughies for YOU

The Times editorial laments
the halcyon era
of cotton tracksuits at the meet
There was a time and a place
Now it's one size fits all
and synthetics are the go

A couple in Las Vegas
were married in their favourites
last month.
Good enough as long as
the elastic holds up.

Junk Food Attack From Outer Space

My wife and I devoured the full menu
of McDonald's last Saturday night.

We drove through against our will
on the way home
from seeing something scary at the pictures.

Hearing a voice as we waited at traffic lights
on the McEvoy Street corner
another horror film started playing out
in the Holden.

There were knives at the throat
threatening to slit our arteries –
pumping stalled with fear –
if we didn't turn left
and through the golden arches.

As the M illuminated the way
to the junk food hell-club
we slid through its left hand lane –
the Holden uncontrollable
down a slippery-slide
of recycled vegetable oil.

We followed instructions
under threat of transmutation
to their planet.

The voice told us to order one of each
and forget the diet.

As usual
we sat in the car park until we had finished
not wishing to spill chocolate thickshake
on the duco or get mayo stains
on the seat.

The kids will never know
of our brush with the aliens.
Lucky they were spared.

We'll never go home from the movies
via McEvoy Street any more.

Early Retirement

Cobwebs spun like rope
locking the wheel
to the mudguard
are more permanent
than the ancient spiders
imagined possible

Steel thick-cut
as a tank's
rumbling indestructible
through forty years
of salty seaside air.

1952 Packard
(in fading grey)
For Sale $3400
Telephone Barry
9319 0998

Tyres are flat
echoing the mood
of the powerful V8
not allowed to run
for ten years.
Vandals have wielded
a weapon to the
windows – cracked
but unbroken

'Arthur, you're so strong.'
'Dorothy, I love you…
Don't mention any of this
to your mother.'
He zips himself up.
Very little damage
was done to the Packard.

'Dad I don't want to go
to school today.'
'Barry, you're bloody lucky
I'm giving you
a lift in the Packard.'
Arthur – distracted –
brakes suddenly to avoid
an oncoming Dodge.
Barry is thrown across
from the back seat
and hits the windscreen.
Very little damage
was done to the Packard.

'Arthur, are you sure
you're all right to drive
in the dark?'
'Oh for God's sake,
Dorothy, don't start.
I'm wearing my thickest
spectacles.'

When Arthur skidded
off the road in the rain
that night he was killed
instantly.
Very little damage
was done to the Packard.

Barry was bequeathed
the Packard
complete with morbid
dent in the front bumper
occasioned when Arthur
came to his fatal rest
as it hit the tree.

Dorothy didn't want him
to hold onto it –
too many memories
Although her mother
never did find out
or wonder why
Barry was three weeks
premature
Such a big baby.

Coffeehouse Chain

Amidst returning tourists
at Circular Quay on dusk,
satisfied with their shopping bags
and holiday,
Beethoven is playing
over the loudspeaker,
straining to reach the high notes
of a cultured retreat.

Polluted by uncleared tables
and thrown-away wrappers,
it isn't making the grade.

The discerning accelerate past,
leaving me to write
the poem in an uncrowded space.

The Lawyers

Language unfathomable
to today's reader
struggles to connect
Mystique maintained
for yet another age
A business protected
with steel walls of words.

Serious accusations
increase the price
of defence
and seem to cause
the wearing of wigs
although it's no party
in the courtroom
If anyone gets drunk
may it not be the judge
on the prosecutor's
fabrications.

Conviction in one's view
convincingly delivered
A jury's dilemma eased.
Defendant is excused
justice served or not.

Some successful,
learned or watched over
by political patrons
inherit gavel
bigger wig
and a lower salary
for power and status
and maybe for virtue.

Precedents into common law
feeding the libraries
bulging with thought –
dusty but ripe
for the next generation
of students.

Motel Room

Bed springs hammered almost limp
by an ever-changing roster of intruders,
deliver me up to the shagpile carpet
in their last dying rebound.

Standing at the basin,
red veins in my eyes
criss-crossing a full view
of a pasty face,
I discover a cracked tile –
the concealed border crossing
to a lost nation of mould.

Usefully I am told in the Service Directory
that I can tantalise my taste buds
at the motel restaurant,
or dial '9' for church or limousine services,
ice, or a florist.

The choice seems endless,
but at dawn all I want
is a cup of tea with milk.

Dust hangs frightened on the curtains
as I wander naked around the room
looking for a lost black sock

In my half-wake I stand staring
at the evacuation procedures –
what curious family would gather
in the grassy square opposite
should a fire break out?

Two lovers wrapped in their sheets,
a hairy belly hanging over fraying boxer shorts,
with others in leather,
a woman in pearls
and me with one sock.

Artist's Studio

Wire-reinforced glass
of the warehouse windows
makes square light in the day
slicing the cylindrical fluorescent glow
from above.

Over a hundred brushes
all sizes and hairstyles
waiting their turn
to dance in the coloured paint.

Three unfinished canvases
calling out for attention in the night
across the cavernous space
drowning out the ghosts
of broken-down engines
from the motor mechanic's workshop
it was.

Old twelve-inch telly
and the CD player
which lets the Pet Shop Boys
and Dionne Warwick
have their say but not interfere.

Thick cool water pipes
criss-crossing the wooden ceiling
will drown any fire
which breaks out
to threaten the stories
hanging on the walls
and stacked in shelves – claustrophobic –
waiting for delivery to the homes
of eager adoptive parents.

Picasso – A Woman Ironing

In her blue-grey state
she could no longer
give herself to the task

Sweat sticking the white
camisole to her exhausted frame.

Graffiti

Politeness and protocol amongst graffitists
means that a magnificently defaced
railway retaining wall –

accessed by the artists
only with the greatest danger –

is divided into many small canvases.

Lines of Communication

A business memorandum
flicked out in shorthand
decipherable only by the team
of code-cracking stenographers

The dwindling local branch
of the Esperanto society
holding to an old dream
sends a letter to its head office
asking if there is a word for 'spam mail'

A famous mime slowly going deaf
wills that more people will learn his craft
so they can reach him
with their messages
in his old age

At Circular Quay in 1933
a Chinese man knew he would fail
the dictation test in Greek.
He spoke Mandarin and English
very skilfully indeed.

A scream rings over the houses
from down the street
A woman no longer able
to protect herself with words
needs someone's help now.

In his maiden speech to parliament
the newly-elected politician sets out
to impress
His colleague – a veteran of five elections –
talks to the people's fears
and mentally counts his retirement fund.

A bride and groom waltz
around the floor without saying a word
giving as much energy
to each other as they can and dare.
Two ancient aunts carry on chatting
right through the vote of thanks,
one gripping her sister's arm
as if to make the conversation
flow right through.

Ten Years

Retrieving memories
like walking blindfolded
backwards through the maze
relies on chance
or is it a sense of direction
given by the past?

Over ten years
detail is lost
then flames vivid
sparked by a recollection
fanned by remembered gusts
of youthful play

At the grave
mourners' footsteps were heavy
on the dry brittle grass
Bagpipes calling us
to cruel attention in the heat

But we have never been alone
despite the loss of him
Bonds have weathered
through each year
and will
We are there again
to see him and talk

Now he is electricity
prodding me to move
Cheers from the sidelines
Answers to a question
A good course steered.

More to us in death
than some could ever be in life

In ten years we have doubted
when science shouted and prevailed

At times we have known
and touched him again

Not the selfishness of
the unrelenting living
but a friendship working
to its limit beyond the
mortal boundaries.

Family Reunion

Great meanderings around everyday topics,
filling in the time and the chasm
between our interests,
patch and sooth the bonds of family.

Photos of grandma and us
spark fierce but soon-forgotten debate
about which holiday it was –
had our old dog already been put down
or was he out of view
cooling himself under the veranda
of the beach house
nursing his arthritis?

Photos of me in the fashionable corduroy suit
made by mum when I was nine
Which cousin's wedding
were we travelling to
when I threw up on it – carsick again.

Over twenty years since the last party
but the genes don't let us forget
how it used to be done.

Siblings all comparing laugh lines –
not so subtly when glasses
are needed to see such distances.

Now-grey hair clearly stating
it's been too long since the last time.

All so badly wanting it to work
to celebrate the patriarch's eighty years
and to close the era of silence.

That Summer

That summer in the share house
was my most crowded.
Eight adults in the three-bed weatherboard –
morning traffic in the hallway
as grumpy and fixated
as commuters through Central Station.

A packet of cereal can't live forever
and the tearing of the carcass
for the last flakes
was in hindsight unseemly,
and poorly planned.

There was money available through magic
for beer and spirits
which flowed for the eight,
their friends and thirsty lovers,
but in rough hung-over dawns
we each felt alone.

A Neptune Man

Stopping to examine a crack in the pavement,
suddenly interesting
Steadying himself on a white picket fence,
useful as moonlight on the difficult drunken track home
Pausing, palms on his half-spread thighs
to draw enough breath not to throw up.

The light fades and there is nothing
Only the blackness holds him upright
His feet shuffle along

Night of friendship and dance
Poisoned by booze
Despatched by the women

Feeling concrete waves under his feet
Getting in too deep
Then a dumper and a crack of bone
Awash with nausea

An old Neptune man visits with long white beard
but ragged clothes
Life held in a shopping trolley
with four plastic bags of history
I know this is your place but I don't need help
I can swim alone
Move away, let me through
I'll drown if I'm with you

Daylight
Head above water,
Taste of blood
Skull in a vice
Dawning of memory

Walking now and wallet and keys intact
What were the odds I wasn't rolled?
The bearded homeless man following
with sardonic gaze
Mind must be shot by metho
Self-respect is what you need
to get you off the streets
Clean yourself up for god's sake
Sorry, mate, no change today

Too early to be seen by anyone
who could harm a reputation
Caffeine and a long shower
and a few lies to the boys
What an event
She wanted me all night
Even hit the head on the end of the bed
Home exhausted at 6 a.m.

Countdown

Excitement of power
and economic control
is cloaked in words
which are spun by doctors
prompting the media
to listen and gorge
on the market
grown hungry by fear.

War is necessary for peace
Forced regime change
is in the name of democracy
Dissent grows quickly amongst
those who cannot acquiesce
in the platitudes of a president
who himself was barely elected

Outrage is incubated and
multiplies through the internet –
out of the control
of governments
which also now prosper
on its ubiquitous talents.

Swimmer In the Sea Baths

Early swimmer
fat as a barrel
Aged like quality red maturing inside
Agitating washing machine
all sideways movement
not even inching ahead.

Waves over the sea wall
impeding progress
Current pushing him back
to the mossy starting barrier.

Routine is a magnet
Chilled winter sea
not a part of the consideration.

Young emerge
seeking cold water on skin
to reverse a Sunday morning hangover
A spontaneous idea with friends
Not yet the repetition
of their old parents.

Chopping Vegies For the Stew

Bert was chopping vegetables at the sink
to bulk up the weekly pot.

It could no longer be called beef stew
with only the few sinews he could afford.

A momentarily unknown noise,
an invasive rap at the door at six pm
by when the shutters of his day
were always well down.

Grandpa, are you there?

Well I think I am
but can I push back
the crushing vice of my old man's night
and pretend to a grandson
that I am not merely
wafting ghost-like
in this oversized house.

Charlton Boys

A minor gay celebrity in the change room
keeps count of those who recognise him
as he slowly pulls on his shorts,
underwear-less pride choking
against the upward zip.

Bright red and blue Speedos
pierce life into the camouflage grey backdrop
of significant ships of the Australian navy.

A lean man in green floral board shorts,
legs folded straight underneath
stretches his neck muscles in yoga style,
giving an alternating view of his neighbours,
whose pecs were all spray-painted
with the same stencil.
Now he lowers his back to the deck,
a sun-tanned double amputee.

In my corner of the bleachers,
a pod of smooth-skinned boys
sleeps off a Saturday morning hangover.
One keeps watch,
and in signals too high for most to receive,
warns his friends when to be alert.

Yogi, legs now returned
pushes his left ankle up toward his neck,
onlookers unsure where it will go next.
Instantly he is a coffee table,
two forearms for legs,
straight back and butt form a top.

In the pool
a chorus line of lap swimmers flawlessly performs
its choreographed freestyle routine.

As the tiring January sun crouches
behind western-side eucalypts,
Charlton boys clothe up for departure,
some in pleasing pairs,
and the filters down below
are left to gargle their solution
of sunscreen and salt water.

The 1960s As Ancient History

Clear memory of situations
by a small child
shriek today's currency
so cannot be ancient

Knowledge kept warm
in girls' beehive hairdos
and today in a computer
Where did men keep it
then?

Girls transformed with fashion:
Maintained with peroxide
and bonnet hair dryer
Miniskirts letting the legs
out for a walk

Boys in dark suits
of single breast
white shirt and thin tie
Simple uniform
of their gender

Today's born say
the sixties was another age
Unwinnable war
fought by a nation
propelled by hallucinogens.

Headlights of Loss

If something should happen to me,
I'll be dead
so it won't matter anyway
except for all the paperwork
and maybe spontaneous tears from a few,
caught off-guard in the headlights of loss.

If something should happen to me
I will never worry or feel pain.
My spirit is there but only
to help you through.
It's not me any more.

If something should happen to me,
I'm at that position in the cycle
where you nourish, fertilise and feed
not eat breathe and speak.
Being a part –
only organic and quiet.

To Write Like Toni Morrison

In *Sula* she wrote about understanding
a poor man escaping pain.

'He'd have to stand in the back
of Greater Saint Matthew's
and let the tenor's voice
dress him in silk.'

Seeing those words
I was all at once wearing silk too.

There is a ruse of simplicity in the writing –
with a punch-in-the-jaw aftertaste.

I want to capture that essence,
sear it into my own expression
and have them turning back
over the pages for another look
and then shiver.

After *Men At Work* – Graham Greene

Deep in the belly of the eight-car snake
like prey resigned to their fate
but dressed up all the same,
commuters were squashed and part-digested
to be extruded out in town.

After *The Loved One* – Evelyn Waugh

Since breakfast the Bondi sun
had been melting beachgoers
but by afternoon it retreated
behind the shopfronts,
searing the paint on west side windows
which stared all day uselessly
at stray cats and garbage in the lane.

After *Dusty Answer* – Rosamund Lehmann

A thick blanket of water
was thrown over the garden.
Its suddenness made the sky change
to grey and those seedlings
which were still standing
were reeling from the punch.

The succulents didn't react
one way or the other –
quite unfazed in their thirst-less world;
and nearby the newly planted herbs
still wondering about their fate
in one of the human's foul-smelling
cooking pots.

The old box hedge – just trimmed back –
gave a stoic performance by the fence.

I'm Sure It Was Jan Morris

Now late back to the office
after a lunch-time stroll down George Street,
the mire of a like-minded crowd
parted to let the tall late-middle-aged lady
have some space.

The confident traveller
with an inquisitive awareness
met my dullard's gaze.

I can only imagine she thought me
a deranged fan.
She knew I recognised her
before I knew it myself.

Then the mire took her back
before I could venture:
'Ms Morris, I love your work.
I'm sorry, it is Ms Jan Morris, isn't it?
Yes, I thought it was. I hope
you don't mind a quick chat.
Apologies for holding you up like this
but I just wanted to ask…'

'No problem, dear. What was it you
needed, some directions?'

Or maybe an invitation to tea
would have ensued, followed by
a lifelong friendship.

Summer Holiday From Writing School

Ideas suppressed
by schoolroom chores
and the drive to publish,
breaking the surface

Straggly weeds
in between the paving blocks,
or a rare wildflower?

Hard to identify
Time will tell us which.

Foreigner Learns Tea

Pleats on the gold silk hakama
need smoothing after time in storage
The grey kimono turning heads
in the Tokyo street.

Water boiling in the iron kettle
resting on the gotoku
over charcoal embers.

Hatsugama is the most
formal of tea ceremonies
The new year ritual affirming
an ancient tradition.

Foreign student of twenty-five years
moves back to his country
drawn by a young culture still unfolding.

Distance is put between him
and his teacher –
now ageing as all

Between visits tea will be served
on the simple roof terrace
of the house by the Sydney sea.

Hakama   divided skirt for men (traditional formal wear)
Gotoku   kettle holder used in tea ceremony
Hatsugama first tea ceremony of the new year

Public Library

There is an incessantly ringing bell
on the information desk
and someone behind me
with a cough – all-consuming –
surely leaving no time
for him to read.

And the one in the corner
summoning inspiration
with every click of his Bic.

There is another staring at me
I'll never know
if it were because of the frozen
pained expression I wore
writing this poem
or my smart outfit
(which my partner said
didn't match).

I don't have a deadline here
Others do.
That's why they look exhausted
unless they never get out
into the sun and fresh air
or eat proper home-cooked food.

Bored and curious glances
cast around the room
like on the council bus
but here there's nobody standing
holding onto the strap as we turn a corner.
The journey is in our heads.

I am happy enough
until the fluorescent light begins
to flicker its annoying picture show
making my erudite friends
start and dance.

I lose my place in the
oversized reference book.

Separation

Burning fear of a separation
allowing no more contact
during remaining mortal time.

In a compartment of my mind
there is a solitary confinement
Release only on my death.

We are told to let go
those invaded by pain
and ready to abdicate life
while there is still dignity.

When there is to be no recovery
other ways will make suffering
prosper for longer than it deserves.

The momentary precipice
confronts me:

In front there is unconsciousness
and death
Time has run out to raise
that which plays on the mind

Behind is a mire
of over-sentimental chatter
and revelation
unnecessary for all

Only the sure-footed can stand
at this place
I don't want to fall either way
but neither are gains made being still.

Phyl and Roy

Phyl

We have a full colour view –
Roy and I –
of our boy
when he's home
and his great pie slice of the Pacific
chopping from blue to green to black
in a rare storm.

Still hard to adjust to being cared for
like this by nature and our son.
The shop was seven days
and eleven hours.
The whole town relied on us to be there.

Long after the shop closed down
we visited Buckingham Palace you know
The boy had connections there.
Very grand for us simple country folk.
Didn't have to think twice
about forking out for a new frock
to go with that fur wrap.
Never in my wildest dreams
would I have got a present like that.

Roy

In the serenity of reflection
I see Phyl and I had a pride
which sometimes we could not show
The time was steeped in our parents' ways
And Mr Menzies was a challenging modern.

Near the end I made it
up those flights of stairs
scaling all the years
of observing at a distance.
Out of breath but finally together.

Now with Phyl again,
a growing palm shades
the long beach holiday
with our young man
and his own love.

Birthday

A celebration in splendid simplicity
in the clear-aired outdoors.

Stereo sound of calm wind brushing ears,
and from the other speaker of nature,
a thousand new waves
breaking their voices on the shore.

Three seagulls in motionless formation,
uplifted by the warm current of sea air,
shifting now to see the view
of a banquet laid out
on the beach house veranda.

They tune to the raucous happiness
of the humans and their birthday guests.

Friendship

In the rear-view mirror,
miles of the sun-coloured road
pass at speed,
dust tufting the scene.

The fullness of the windscreen
unfolds mystery of travel and friends,
keepers of the world's languages.

A classical education
seared into the mind
with cold showers
in the winter of Geelong
and the kindnesses
and mischievous experiments
of a rower's youth.

Humour and love,
anti-venene of the Scorpioni's sting
sustain us in a sweet friendship.

Bagpipes play across the tradition of family
and announce his presence
to the valley and the sky.

When Your Lover Is Happy

Lapping of warm clear tropical sea
enlivened by small inquisitive fish
nibbling at your toes,
begging some attention
and unafraid.

Big steady ships
passing in the distance
become one.

Ten-foot waves
which will drown a man
are invisible from here.

When Your Lover Is Unhappy

Caught in the unending onslaught
of a powerful sea at night
Surf pushing and pulling the legs
from under you.

No moonlight or Mars
to show the way out.

Ships are steaming in opposite directions
silent from here in the crashing
of the waves.

Lord, bring on the morning.

Au Revoir

The telephone conversation
you had planned to be our last –
goodbye with welling of tears
and then the line was dead

You were too strong
to succumb to your cocktail
of resolution

They said regaining yourself
would take time

See beauty in small things –
like even the oppressed do.
There is enough to share.

Six months of repair and reflection
could not change your mind
in the blackest night

We try to understand
and laugh and reach you

Delicate Child of Day

On the western coast
the old woman of the sea
embraces the clear blue day
and welcomes it inside.

She serves it warm milk
and a story.
Time to be tucked in
and a kiss goodnight –
a delicate beautiful child
on a regular sleepover.

Sunset,
then a fresh beginning.

www.ingramcontent.com/pod-product-compliance
Lightning Source LLC
Chambersburg PA
CBHW062148100526
44589CB00014B/1733